Michael Winicott

LINKEDIN:
JOB SEARCH AND CAREER BUILDING

How to Use LinkedIn for Employment and Career Branding

UNITEXTO
Digital Publishing

1

Table of Contents

INTRODUCTION: WHAT IS LINKEDIN?

When it comes to social networking, chances are that you may be using at least one or two or more social networking sites to keep yourself informed on your friends' activities and to check what's new on networks you follow. If you are presently employed and not using LinkedIn as a tool to connect and stay updated with people, companies and groups in your industry, you are committing a serious mistake. It's time to reconsider your view of professional networking.

Being the world's largest networking site for professionals, LinkedIn is an innovative way to connect with people in almost any industry. It is the most powerful tool of modern age to create and manage your professional identity and brand your career. It gives you opportunities to connect and engage with professionals, and access knowledge, insights and opportunities. LinkedIn keeps you informed about your contact and industry and helps you find the people and knowledge you need to achieve your professional goals.

There is a serious misconception that LinkedIn is only for people seeking job. With almost 347 million LinkedIn users worldwide, we can honestly say the not even 50 percent of them are vigorously looking out for employment. A majority of these users are employed and networking to stay on top of their career.

CHAPTER 1: WHY YOU SHOULD USE LINKEDIN?

According to a study conducted by Jobvite in 2014, there were 94 percent of active recruiters on LinkedIn, and only 36 percent of job seekers. Moreover, a majority of the recruiters said they do most of the hiring through LinkedIn. These facts reinforce the theory that the traditional ways of recruitment are fading and employers are increasingly using innovative ways like LinkedIn to find and recruit talent.

Not only is LinkedIn a tool for effective recruitment for employers, it is also a tool for job seekers to find their dream job. However, this does not mean that the function of LinkedIn is limited to job search and recruitment. It is a complete career branding kit. Read on to know how.

CREATING A WIDE NETWORK TO USE LATER

Creating a profile on LinkedIn now, actively participating and building a strong network can not only be enjoyable, but can also help you in

6

furthering your professional goals at some point in your career. Imagine for a moment that you got fired from your current job; suddenly you realize the importance of LinkedIn. So you create a profile on LinkedIn in a hurry and start adding people to your network like wild.

If LinkedIn doesn't catch you for doubtful behavior, then the hordes of new people you are trying to add to your network may question your purpose. They might ask, "Well, I have not heard from this person in almost a decade, and now suddenly he has been laid off and wants to connect. What is his intention?"

This reinforces the importance of creating a large network on LinkedIn and staying connected even if you are happily employed. Don't wait to join the network until you are in need. Participate actively. Show your connections that you really know how to do things in your industry. Keep in touch.

BETTER OPPORTUNITIES COME TO THOSE WHO ARE ALREADY EMPLOYED

A majority of employers on LinkedIn try to recruit people who are already employed or people who are not actively looking for job. This is understandable, given that there are enough jobless people in the country, and on LinkedIn. What they want is someone who can provide value, has the skills, and is not actively looking for employment.

Your profile on LinkedIn is something recruiters would check to see if you have the necessary skills, experience and knowledge for the vacant position.

In other words, recruiting companies try to pilfer and snatch valuable professionals from their competitors. When they approach you, they are obviously eager to offer your more in terms of money and professional growth. By not being on LinkedIn, you are missing the chance to be discovered by better companies that offer more growth and development opportunities, and of course more money.

GROUPS ON LINKEDIN OFFER YOU CONNECTIONS AND OPPORTUNITIES

Joining your industry groups on LinkedIn can give you access to connections and opportunities. You can find engaging discussions over topics of your interest and can speak your mind. If you provide value to the group and demonstrate your knowledge and skills, you will find more connections and opportunities will come to you.

KEEPING YOUR PROFILE UPDATED BRINGS YOU OPPORTUNITIES

As recruitment is gradually taking innovative turns and steadily more employers are shifting to LinkedIn to find talent, keeping your profile updated will let potential employers to find and contact you. Remember, resume is a static, old thing now. You use it only when you are actively looking for an employment.

On the contrary, you keep your LinkedIn profile updated no matter if you are looking for opportunities or not. Employers are well aware that your LinkedIn profile is more accurate than your resume. You never know when your current employer would stop loving you, so keep your

9

LinkedIn profile updated. It will also help you in updating your resume.

LINKEDIN BRINGS YOU CUSTOMIZED NEWS AND UPDATES FROM YOUR INDUSTRY

LinkedIn can keep you on top of updates and news in your industry. The network offers you the opportunity to regularly get customized news feeds, articles and updates about your industry. Armed with the updated information, you can leap far ahead of other competing candidates in any potential job interview. In other words, LinkedIn builds your talent, so you can grow and develop professionally.

CHAPTER 2:HOW LINKEDIN IS USED FOR JOB SEARCH AND PERSONNEL RECRUITING?

LinkedIn is a very useful and powerful network for every employed individual; let alone every job seeker and student. However, the bad news is that not every casual LinkedIn user is aware of its power as a job-search tool.

If you are updating your LinkedIn profile from time to time and then waiting for potential employers to recruit you, you are missing the opportunity. This tool has a huge database containing millions of records crucial to the job-hunting strategy of every user.

For example, a big company opened up its office in your area and you are curious if they need someone with skills and experience like you. The traditional ways of calling or writing to the company's HR department are no more workable.

There is this powerful tool called LinkedIn that would help ease your tedious task. Just log in to your LinkedIn network, go to the company's profile and there you see some of your friends and connections already working in your target company. Now you can reach out to your connections working there to get all information on any openings. Smart job, but this is not all.

Now you go to the LinkedIn profiles of the company's top management and there you find that one of them went to your graduate alma mater.

Here is the good news: your Alumni Office can help you get it touch with him or her if you think personally approaching him would not be the right way. You also find that one of the company's executives is a board member of a non-profit organization where your friend's mom is an executive. Now you can use this connection to your advantage as well.

CHAPTER 3: BUILDING A KILLER PROFILE

Your LinkedIn profile is a tool to broadcast your strengths, skills, achievements, competencies, talent and future aspirations. Additionally, it is a tool to make first impression to anyone who finds you on the network, be it a past or future colleague intending to connect with you, a prospective client, or a potential employer. Understanding the importance of a killer profile is good, but more important is to know where to begin and what information to put up. It can be somehow daunting at the outset.

Here are some tips to build a killer profile on LinkedIn:

1. **Add headline:** LinkedIn would ask you to write a headline. Write a headline that catches the attention of people. It should mention the industry you work in and communicate what you are best at.

2. **Publish posts:** Publishing posts is a great way of building a profile that gains exposure

and gets noticed by people in your network and industry. Stay in by posting your publications on your profile, sharing relevant and helpful articles and information, and posting updates pertaining to your industry.

3. **Write summary:** While building your profile, LinkedIn would ask you to write a professional summary. Never ignore it because it is the key to build a killer profile. Briefly narrate the companies you have worked for, mention major projects you have accomplished and don't forget to include keywords in your summary, so people can easily discover you in searches.

4. **Add your experiences:** Add your work experiences to make your profile shine and let potential employers and connections see what you do, what you are best at and what are your achievements. Be precise, but don't be afraid to use important details, such as your achievements on the positions you held and your job responsibilities.

5. **Add your skills:** Adding your skills to your profile would tell potential employers what you are best at. If you have already added your skills on your LinkedIn profile, update them as you gain more skills through trainings and development programs. Don't forget to add keywords, so people can easily find you based on your skills. You can even request your colleagues and connections for endorsement of your skills. Endorsements from your connections will show alongside your skills.

6. **Join relevant groups:** When you join a group on LinkedIn, it shows up on your profile. This will let your connections and potential employers see that you are actively participating in relevant groups and are well informed about your industry.

7. **Add volunteer experience and causes:** While building your LinkedIn profile, the network would prompt you to add volunteer experience and causes you care about. If you have volunteer experience, don't hesitate to add it. This tells your potential employer and connections that you are a real human being

who has feelings and cares about things. Some examples of causes include the environment, children, education, social services and senior citizens. You can even add the organizations you support that are working for the causes you care about.

8. **Add education:** Adding education to your LinkedIn profile is as important as it is in your resume. Your education tells your connections and potential employers that you have the required talent, are well groomed, and have the skills to do certain tasks. For example, if you have done MBA, add it to your education with the degree's starting and ending dates in addition to the school you earned the degree from. Be specific while adding your education.

9. **Add project:** Never hesitate to add the projects you worked on as a team member or leader. You can even add other colleagues who worked on the project team to show on your profile. This would broadcast your achievements and talent.

10. **Add publications:** Publications don't necessarily mean you have to write books, so you can add them to your profile. If you already have written a book, it's time to show it off on your LinkedIn profile. If you haven't, you can add researches you did, even if it was a university dissertation, articles you wrote for any website, blogs you wrote, and anything you produced that is relevant to your industry.

11. **Recommendations:** Recommendations are very powerful when it comes to getting a job via LinkedIn and you should have them on your profile. They show unbiased reviews of your performance and your work attitude, and establish your core competencies. Even though, recommendation can only be displayed for the particular positions you held and schools you received your education from, yet they still possess conversion potency.

    Request your supervisors, colleagues, teachers and classmates for recommendations on LinkedIn and make sure to display them on your profile. You

17

have the option to hide bad recommendations and keep the positive ones only. Potential employees see recommendations to know how you performed on the positions you held.

CHAPTER 4: NETWORK, NETWORK, NETWORK

Once your killer profile is up and running, it's time to network. Networking is the key to success. Without proper networking, your efforts will go in vain and you will fail to get noticed. You can start by connecting with existing professionals you know and personal connections, such as friends, past colleagues, present co-workers, and classmates.

We meet and interact with dozens of people in our work and personal lives, and it is always wise to stay in touch with people you have good interaction with. The best way to do this is to add him or her on LinkedIn.

Some people would send you invitation to connect, and if you think that you don't know them personally, don't ignore it altogether. Sometimes, they can be potential employers or clients and maybe someone who is working in your industry and is impressed by your profile and participations. They can be of great help in future.

Before sending people invitation to connect, stop

19

and think for a while. It is not a good gesture to connect with anyone randomly. If you come across someone you don't know, but could be helpful in furthering your career goals, don't add them by sending generic message like "Hi, I would like to connect with you on LinkedIn."

Remember, everyone has unique way of perceiving requests to connect and using LinkedIn. Some people use LinkedIn to only stay in touch with people they've met offline. You should always write some details about yourself in your message, introduce yourself and tell why you want to connect with him or her.

Here are some tips you can use to increase your LinkedIn connections:

Experiences bring connections: Sometimes we are more experienced than we realize. Experience is more important in increasing your connections; therefore, think broadly about all your experiences, such as internships you did, volunteer experiences, and student organizations you worked in. We never know what might attract someone's attention.

A complete profile: Profiles that are 100 percent have relatively 40 times more chances of getting connections. Remember, people are more interested in what you have to offer and that comes from a complete profile.

Using your inbox: Using your LinkedIn inbox is a powerful tool to bring in more connections because networking is not about always sending cold connection requests to complete strangers. You can even upload your online address book from your email account to connect with people you know.

Getting friendly: While sending connection request, be friendly. It is better to send a reminder about where you met, when you met and how you met. If you haven't met, you may have a common organization or a cause you both care about. This approach will increase your chances of having more connections.

Finding connections in groups: LinkedIn groups are great way of finding new connections. You can start by joining your school group, alumni group or volunteer organization you worked for. Another great way is to join groups that are related to the industry you work in.

Supporting others: Lending a helping hand and supporting other can bring you new connections. Commenting on or sharing a potential connection's post can be returned with generosity.

Status updates: Remember, LinkedIn networking is not completely about who you know; it is equally about who knows you. Post frequent status updates to stay on the radar of others. You should post relevant updates. For example, it is better to post about reading a book of innovative marketing strategies if you are in that industry rather than about a romance novel.

Using an appropriate image on your profile: Using an appropriate profile image can impress people and bring more connections. It should be your own picture with a smiling face.

CHAPTER 5: FIND A JOB AND GET IT

If used wisely, LinkedIn offers you great opportunities to find your dream job. Here are some tips on how to find a job on LinkedIn and get it:

1. **Jobs board:** LinkedIn maintains a dedicated jobs section where employers post their jobs. It is a good idea to start searching for a relevant job on the dedicated section. The good news is that you can see the complete job description right on LinkedIn. You can even apply for the job by clicking the "Apply Now" tab using your LinkedIn profile as your resume. You also get the option to upload your resume or cover letter.

2. **Using the search function:** You can use the search bar showing at the top of the LinkedIn website to find a relevant job you may want to apply for. Use proper and relevant keywords to find opportunities. For example, if you type in "Telecom Engineer Career," the system will respond by

returning a list of available opportunities in telecom engineering, related groups, and people who are doing similar jobs.

3. **Importance of profile:** You can find your dream job on LinkedIn, but that doesn't mean you can get it for sure. To maximize your chances of getting the job, you need to have a complete LinkedIn profile. Prospective employers would see your profile once you apply for a job. If your profile is incomplete or lacks basic and important information, you chances of being called for an interview diminishes. Therefore, make sure that you have a complete profile.

4. **Joining relevant groups:** Groups are the windows to opportunities. Find relevant groups, join them and participate to get yourself noticed by members. You never know one of the members might be the CEO of a company in your industry; seeing your serious contribution and participation in the group may make him consider you for a vacant position in his company.

5. **Connections:** Connections are important in many ways, including their potential to get you hired. Regularly check into LinkedIn to see what your connections have posted. You may find a job opening posted by a connection and it could be one you are looking out for. Grab the opportunity and send a message to your friend indicating your interest in the job. You should also keep yourself in by regularly posting updates, and interesting and helpful materials. This will keep you on the radar of your connections and whenever there is a relevant opening, chances are that they will get to you.

CHAPTER 6: BUILDING A CAREER WITH LINKEDIN

Your professional branding on the Internet is very important in today's world and LinkedIn is the key to it. If used properly, LinkedIn can be a powerful and effective tool to build and manage your professional brand. The question is: how to use it properly and effectively?

Here's how.

1. **Be genuine:** If you want to be the best LinkedIn identity, you have to be authentic, honest, and keep the light on factors that make you unique, and values you have the ability to offer. Remember, branding your career is not like a spin.

2. **Shun clichés:** Some words are too common and meaningless on LinkedIn, such as team player, vast experience, creative etc. When describing your skills, accomplishment and experience, use unique words and ways.

3. **Stay visible:** Professional branding won't work if you create a profile and then just

26

wait for your connections to respond. It requires you to do things that would keep you on the radar of other people. You can do this by updating your status with your current projects, books and publications you are reading, professional gatherings you are attending, and your excitement about challenging tasks you are doing on your current position. Remember, your professional brand is not just who you are, but also what you do.

4. **Brand connection:** Just like in real life you are judged by the company you keep, on LinkedIn people judge you by the connections you keep. Connect with relevant, talented and skilful people, especially people from your industry.

5. **Broadcast your knowledge:** You may have a knack for programming, but if you don't let your network know about it, you are missing opportunities. To stay on top of your career, always distinguish yourself by knowing and promoting your work religiously. You can do

this by posting status updates on your current projects and their dynamics.

With more than347 million members across the world, LinkedIn is the largest go-to career resource for professional branding. You can manage your professional identity on LinkedIn by:

- Using the tool to keep eye on where others with your major are currently working.

- Going to the tool to discover connections for informational interviews.

- Using the directory to find job leads.

- Going to company pages to search companies, find opportunities and connect with their employees.

- Using LinkedIn Pulse to stay up-to-date on news and happenings in a career or industry.

- Going to career-specific groups and participating in discussion with people sharing your interests.

CHAPTER 7:
TIPS AND TRICKS

- Customize your public profile URL by removing the confusing digits from the URL and adding a custom name. You can do this by clicking here and modifying the URL on the top right corner.

- Make your profile shine by adding a background photo. You can do this by clicking on Profile >> Edit Profile in LinkedIn's top navigation and then clicking Add a background photo at the top of your page.

- Add relevant keywords in your skills, experiences, summary and headline to get found by others looking for people like you.

- Add media like pictures, videos, documents, presentations and publications to showcase your work and the projects you have completed.

- User LinkedIn's job directory to search and find relevant jobs.

- Write catchy headlines on your profile, and add summary briefly describing you experiences and skills.

- Add experiences and ask for recommendations.

- Add your skills and get endorsed for them.

- Don't add people coldly. Introduce yourself; tell him or her where and when you met and show interest in his or her work to get accepted.

- Check your LinkedIn account regularly to keep eye on opportunities.

- Post regular status updated to get noticed. Avoid spamming.

- LinkedIn gives you the option to see who has viewed your profile. This would give you indications about people's interest in you and your work.

- Join and engage in relevant groups to find opportunities, get connections and brand your career.

CONCLUSION

With more than 347 million users worldwide, LinkedIn has turned onto a powerful tool to search and find jobs, build and manage your professional brand and stay updated about your industry. To use this tool to its full potential, you need to know how it works. Creating a profile is just the tip of the iceberg. There's a lot more to it.

Never neglect your LinkedIn profile if you are not actively seeking a job. LinkedIn is a complete career-branding tool, not just a job search portal. It gives you dozens of options to stay on top in your industry and current job. It brings you valuable resources and lets you interact with connections. It gives you the option to join and participate in groups to enhance your talent. And of course, the key to success on LinkedIn is building a killer profile.

When it comes to finding connections on LinkedIn, do not just randomly add people. The best way is to find people you know or you've met, and then send them a connect request with a personal message that should introduce you, describe where and when you met and show your interest in the other's work. If you want to add someone you don't know, add him or her with a personal message introducing you are and explaining why you want to connect.

Stand out from the crowd by making a unique profile. Use words that are unique to describe your skills, experiences and accomplishments.

Your headline and summary are the most important things on your profile. Make sure to have creative headline and summary that shall communicate what you do, and briefly narrate your skills.

The best place to search and find a job is LinkedIn's job portal. Visit the job portal regularly to see opportunities. You can apply for jobs right from LinkedIn using your LinkedIn profile.

Regularly posting status updated will get you noticed and may bring you an opportunity. And keeping an eye on status updates of your connections can bring you an opportunity too.

Happy career branding with LinkedIn!

BOOKS FROM MICHAEL WINICOTT

Another titles by Michael Winicott you may find interesting:

BILL GATES: BUSINESS LESSONS

BRAIN: EXERCISES TO EMPOWER

BUSINESS PLAN: A practical guide

FACEBOOK MARKETING: Business Lessons from Mark Zuckerberg

HABITS: MICRO CHANGES for MACRO RESULTS

HENRY FORD: ENTERPRENEURSHIP LESSONS

JESUS: LEADERSHIP LESSONS

LEONARDO DA VINCI: CREATIVITY LESSONS

MARTIN LUTHER KING: LIFE LESSONS

OPRAH WINFREY: LIFE LESSONS

STEVE JOBS: BUSINESS LESSONS

WALT DISNEY: CREATIVITY LESSONS

WINSTON CHURCHILL: LEADERSHIP LESSONS

DID YOU ENJOY THIS BOOK?

Thanks for purchasing and reading this book.If you reached this page you had probably enjoyed it.Would you care to leave a positive review in Amazon?

This is very important for 2 reasons:

a) I need your feedback to improve the quality of my books

b) Other people may read and benefit from this book if you share your thoughts.

CPSIA information can be obtained
at www.ICGtesting.com
Printed in the USA
LVHW021454120123
736951LV00003B/828

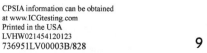

9 781514 861820